We Thought You Knew

By Philippa Gerry

Contents

Introduction

Acknowledgements

This is for Simon, who kickstarted it, Anne, who spent hours making it grow, and Andrew, who at the right moment told me to read Children of the Raj. Since the East India Company and before, hundreds of European men have gone to seek their fortune in India: in the Army, in the Indian Civil Service, in commerce, as missionaries and as planters like my father. Wives and families meant questions of what was best for the children. Even today, the dilemma is still there for families going to live abroad, involved in the Forces, in NGOs, in peace keeping, charity workers, mine clearers, and many more. Mothers of the Raj could be an interesting research project.

How it began.

Our vicar, Simon, said he would talk about me, but not till my funeral for fear I might sue him. I told him I would put a big C for copyright on my wicker coffin. So there. When my daughter Katherine heard of this, she laughed like a drain. If she is at my funeral, she can tell me about it afterwards (sending messages up and down as the case may be). So, Simon, here is ammunition for you, or explanation.

What it is

It's a story about what happens when people don't communicate. It is an attempt to understand what happened, why, so as to know how to prevent muddles. "We live life forwards; we understand it backwards." Is it truthful? I hope so. It is the best I can. Has writing it helped me? Emphatically yes. "Tout comprendre c'est tout pardonner." Everyone struggles with something. My struggle has been with a lifelong fear of rejection. I go rigid with completely unnecessary fear. "All behaviour is learned." Therefore, behaviour can be unlearned or re-learned. One hopes. "Perfect love casts out fear". Even imperfect love is a big help. In fact, the little unbreakable golden thread which has brought me out of the labyrinth away from the minotaur has been the love of God, shown in nature, in animals, in the love of family, of friends, sitting there wagging its tail, hoping to be noticed.

India

The first five years of my life were wonderful. In the early 1930's
Daddy (Howard Gerry), Mummy (Molly Gerry) and I (Philippa)
lived in the spacious bungalow my father had built on the edge
of the tea estate he managed for Brooke Bond. It was in the
Arnamullai Hills in South India. He had up to 2000 estate workers
plus their dependents in his care. It was a responsible job which
he loved.

My mother had all the time in the world for me. There were
cooks, house servants, a gardener and an ayah. We were almost
completely cut off from the outside world. The jungle came right
up to our house on one side of the long dirt drive. On the other
side the tea plantation stretched down the hill. The nearest
neighbours – also tea planters – were two miles away. Groceries
came from a nearby village. The post was fetched on foot by one
of the coolies. It was a walk of several miles. The coolies fought
to have this job.

My memories of that time are fragmented and not always clear
but it seemed to me to be heaven. I can remember either blazing
sunshine or lashing monsoon rain. Ayah and I walked down the
jungle path to watch the elephants relaxing in the river, spraying
their mahouts, themselves, and each other with water using
their trunks. I remember a rolling ride high on an elephant's back
and monkeys in the tall trees. We walked back. I tugged ayah's
hand. "Look, pussy cat!" An interested tiger was sitting upright
on a log about eight feet away. We ran.

I remember times when the barefoot bangle man would call. He
brought with him a hessian sack filled with rich objects of many

coloured glass or pre-bakelite bangles. Sometimes there were parties at the tea-planters' club. I was delighted with my fancy dress – a pink tutu with wings but I was miffed when I saw that Bunty and Susan, who were a bit older, very pretty in blue and white tutus, were allowed wands as well. I adored my parents. I had privately decided that my life's work would be to look after both of them for ever. Mummy was my all: best friend, confidant, protector, guide, source of wisdom. Her word was law. I was obedience itself. We were utterly happy.

In 1936 Daddy was due to go on leave. Mummy and I went on ahead. We took the boat from Cochin. The voyage was a new adventure. There was a canvas swimming pool on deck to cool off in the heat. Everyone had ice-cream for elevenses. As we were going through the Suez Canal I was standing beside my mother on the deck and she told me that it was customary to throw one's topee overboard. We ceremoniously took off our sweat-stained pith helmets and flung them over the stern. They bobbed about for a bit and then slowly sank. I remember thinking that Suez must have been full of topees. In the Mediterranean it was cooler. There was lovely hot tomato soup for elevenses. Once Mummy woke me to look out of the porthole to see the volcano Stromboli erupting just off the foot of Italy – red fire in a dark night.

Oldway

In cool autumnal England, we stayed with Mummy's widowed mother – Granny – in her large 1840s red brick house, Oldway, on the edge of Wellington in Somerset. Her husband, Thomas Fox – my grandfather – had died in 1924. He had been a Director of Fox Brothers' woollen mill, then the largest employer in town. They made Fox's Puttees for the entire British army in World War 1. After her husband's death, she stayed on. She had a cook, a parlour-maid, a gardener and a chauffeur-handyman. The house was light and airy. It smelled of scrubbed pine and lavender. In the Morning Room she had bunches of dried flowers. There was a large garden with a tennis court at the front, a lawn and a pond at the side, a paddock where Mummy had kept her pony, and a fantastic walled Victorian kitchen garden. Granny's hobby was making miniature Japanese gardens which she sold for the Church Missionary Society at bazaars.

Their Christian faith meant everything to Granny and Grandfather. At one time he had wanted to be a missionary but had been persuaded to join the family firm instead. When I was only six months old my grandmother made me a Life Governor of the CMS. I still have the certificate, but never had any duties. She was great friends with the then curate.

Granny welcomed us warmly. That autumn I went to an infants' school in a nearby bungalow with Miss Gladys Applin. At the end of term everyone got a prize. At home a great fuss was made of me. Mummy loved dressing me. She bought me a small fur coat with large fur buttons. It was in the middle of the depression but there were no signs of it at Oldway. I had my tonsils out at Wellington Cottage Hospital and a toe removed. A bang on a stone in India had made the toe grow right past the big one, so the surgeon took the whole toe off (they wouldn't do that now). I was given a teddy bear and Walter, the chauffeur, wheeled me round grandly in a bath chair for a bit. In the winter I had bronchitis. I had hot antiphlogistine poultices slapped on my chest and was spoilt rotten with mashed banana and Radio Malt. It was delicious. On Sundays we went to church. Half of my weekly pocket money, which was 2d - went into the collection, leaving me with 1d. As I lacked nothing, I had no need of it. Life was wonderful. I loved and was loved. I was safe and cherished. All this was to change without warning.

Gerbestone Manor

When Daddy arrived from India, he and Mummy would go away for weekends leaving me in the care of Helen, a baby sitter, who was kind and looked like a princess with glorious auburn hair. Granny was always there.

One weekend, however, instead of leaving me at Oldway, they took me to stay at nearby Gerbestone Manor. I hadn't stayed there before. It was the home of Mummy's first cousin, Lloyd Fox – Uncle Lloyd – and his wife Griselda – Aunty G. There was Nanny in an upstairs nursery where my youngest cousin, Penelope and I had tea. Penelope was two years older than me.

After the weekend I put on the navy-blue school uniform Nanny had set out for me. I went down for breakfast. As I walked across the large faded Persian carpet towards the breakfast table where Aunty G and Uncle Lloyd were already sitting, it hit me - this hadn't been just for the weekend. Mummy and Daddy had left for India without me and without telling me they were going. Why? The week before we had been a happy family. Didn't they want me anymore? They must have told other people they were going but not me. All this rushed through my mind as I walked over the last two yards of carpet. I was shocked, silent. I sat there paralysed and numb. I ate what was in front of me - porridge and toast.

 Uncle Lloyd dropped Penelope and me off at the school gates on his way to work. We were day girls at St Katherine's, a Woodard boarding school halfway between Wellington and Taunton. At break, one of the boarders asked me kindly, "Where do your parents live?"

"India."

 For days I was very quiet. I noticed that my toy cupboard and clothes were there. They must have been brought ahead of time in a planned departure. Before I had been a happy bubbling child but now I wasn't. The bottom had fallen out of everything. Mummy had always been there to talk to me and explain things, to tell me what to do and what not to do. Now none of that was there. I loved her. Didn't she want me to love her anymore? Why? What did she want me to do? Aunty G, observing this new child in her care, thought she spied sulks. I think, preoccupied as I was, I must have off handedly said something. I seem to remember saying "No" when offered an orange instead of "No, thank you." Aunty G exploded.

"You're spoilt".

"Oh, spoilt". What did that mean? Spoilt or not, I was bereft. The best mother in the world had just gone away without a word. We had been a happy family, hadn't we? Perhaps there was something wrong with me. Spoilt. I imagined they had found I got in the way, and that they were having a lovely time in India, free of me. Much as it hurt, I wished them well. It was a bad start. It set the tone for everything that followed: Aunty G seeing me as spoilt and me scared. Perhaps my parents had told her to be cross. (What things children imagine). After this, wild horses would not have made me talk to her or ask her to explain. She was a strong character. She ruled Uncle Lloyd (he liked it), us, and the whole household. She used to call it "an iron hand in a velvet glove". As we grew older, we became aware of her work with organisations in the community. How different she was in this from my quiet mother whose life was centred on the home. Aunty G loved the W.I. She became county chair much later. She took me with her one day. It was like a royal progress through W.I.s in North Somerset. For several years she wrote the Country Diary for the Guardian.

Although I wanted to die, life happened one day after another. My parents had said nothing. Aunty G had said nothing. So I obediently said nothing. One of my cousins quoted to me "Children should be seen and not heard." With no Mummy to govern every aspect of my life, I tried to fit in, making myself, I thought, as invisible as possible. I scraped carrots and peeled potatoes for Norah, the cook, in the kitchen. It was warm and safe from Aunty G, who never went in there. Norah was grateful as she had lots to do on her own. I picked plantains for the rabbit in his cage. I collected new-laid eggs which the hens left with much cackling here and there in the hedges. I shut the chickens up at night to keep them safe. With the others, I helped with the children's jobs on the farm.

At about age six, I learned to read. From there on, I read and read. A bookworm was born. When I was about eight, Granny gave me a big grown up dictionary, a Chambers. She herself wrote poems, and a book to comfort people who had lost someone in the War. We had many children's classics: all the Arthur Ransome books, Babar, Beatrix Potter, A A Milne. By about eleven and twelve I was reading Scott, Thackeray and Dickens. There was safety in books. In English classes I was teacher's pet, chosen for the big parts when we read Shakespeare out loud. Wonderful.

My small cold bedroom next to the cook's faced north, looking over the kitchen garden. That winter, there was ice inside the windows – so different from India. I got into my rumpled school uniform under the bedclothes for warmth. With no one to hear, I cried myself to sleep on and off for years. Wonderfully, two half-grown ginger kittens Mac and Sandy found their way to my room. Purring contentedly, they fell asleep. One snuggled in the crook of my knees under the blankets. The other lay firmly on my face with my breath whiffling through his fur. They left at dawn. Knowing this wasn't allowed, I told no one. Almost instinctively I had become secretive to protect myself.

My behaviour sent out small signals of distress which were dealt with but not dealt with. These might have increased Aunty G's impatience with me as a 'problem child'. I bit my nails so they sent me to school in gloves which stopped that. I crept down the curly oak back stairs after bedtime to snitch sugar lumps from the silver bowl. Aunty G caught me and scolded me. "I won't tell Uncle Lloyd". Every time there was a big tea party, I stuffed and stuffed myself with all the varieties of cake till I got a splitting headache and was sick. And, shamefully, I even masturbated when shock and loneliness prevented sleep. I hated myself for all this. None of it brought back my mother.

 Seeing me sad, Uncle Lloyd used to tease me. "The elephants round your father's table are less hard done by than you are." He said it with great humour as an enormous joke. I loved the mental picture plus the mention that I had a father. If Aunty G had been like that, I might even have plucked up courage to ask why my parents had left without saying anything to me.

There were also good things. The beauty of the house, the variety of animals, and nature around it were a great consolation. The house had ten bedrooms, three staircases, a priest's hole, and a supposed secret passage to West Buckland church. There were oak beams, huge fireplaces, inglenooks, and mullioned windows. The property's history went back to the Domesday Book. It was beside an old packhorse lane that ran from Bridgwater to the south coast, a remnant of the lane went up beside the biggest orchard.

I enjoyed helping with the jobs on the farm throughout the year. We made hay and harvested oats, barley, wheat, mangold wurzels and sugar beets. We collected rotten apples into sacks, taking care not to disturb sleepy wasps, to be taken to the Norton Fitzwarren Cider Factory. We threw stones into hedges to clear fields so the ploughshares wouldn't be blunted. We watched the sheep dipping and shearing. We helped feed an

orphan lamb now and then. We chased errant bullocks. They
usually got out on Sunday afternoons which was when we sawed
wood. We cleaned out the swimming pool every spring. We
picked primroses up the lane for children in Great Ormond Street
Hospital. The rest of the time we just played in the gardens,
orchards, wood or around the mill pond. We went to the wood,
full of bluebells, to play at Robin Hood and his merry men.

In the house, life was busy too. Nanny – bless her – loved us all
equally. She supervised us in a balance of homework, board
games, listening to the wireless (ITMA and 'Much Binding in the
Marsh' were favourites), making Christmas paper chains and
presents, and so on. Sometimes I would have liked to be less
busy, to be allowed to think about my parents.

School was good. The teachers were kind. Miss Hartnell, the
head mistress, perceptively saw I was upset and so was extra
nice to me. I was often top or second in English but the last to be
chosen for rounders.

My cousins were Angela and David, who were away at boarding
school most of the time, and Mary and Penelope. When Angela
and David were at home for the holidays we played games all
together. There were fierce frantic contests of Racing Demon
with David going all out to win. In Monopoly he used many tricks
to obtain Mayfair and Park Lane so as to bankrupt everyone else.
There was a game called Milestones, which I hated, a board
game that led players through stages of life from birth (the stork)
to a rest home. The others managed it so that they got married.
I, the odd one out, had to be spinster Aunt Lucy. At which point I

would burst into tears and stalk out. It was the only time they tried to wind me up. It became a family joke.

Games and parties were big at Gerbestone. Aunty G's parties were famous. She loved sharing her house with groups such as the W.I. There were garden parties and indoor concerts. The old house glowed for her fabulous Christmas parties. Before Christmas she put on little children's plays for an audience of family, starring us. We loved it. In 'The Tailor of Gloucester', Mary was the handsome tailor, Penelope and I were the mice, asking for "more twist". Another year it was Charles Kingsley's 'Water Babies', with singing. Although Uncle Lloyd and Aunty G were teetotal, being Quakers, the huntin', shootin' and fishin' people loved to be invited.

 Quaker Meeting in Wellington was a lovely quiet time. Sometimes I went with the family. On other Sundays I was tidied up and dispatched to Granny. She led me very gently into the Christian faith which was everything to her. My happiest, best, most peaceful three weeks of those years in Wellington was when Granny took me to stay with her in a guest house, Applehayes, in the Blackdown Hills. In the mornings she taught me the names of wild flowers in the hedgerows. In the evenings she played card games with me – just her and me. She was the one who talked to me about Mummy.

Slowly the hurt got a little bit less. My life filled up.

Gerbestone Manor in Wartime

When war was declared on September 3rd 1939, we returned rapidly from a holiday in Scotland. The first evacuee was on the doorstep. When the bombing of the big cities began, many more evacuees came to Wellington. Aunty G was billeting officer. I don't know whether she was the chief officer; certainly, it kept her very busy. Among the evacuees there were a number of hard to place ones. These were taken by Uncle Lloyd and Aunty G who had a big barn which they turned into a camp for up to twenty children at a time – girls sleeping upstairs, boys in the main barn. During the whole war, there were sixty altogether as some reached sixteen and left and younger ones took their place. Six, from a family of thirteen, arrived after the bombing of Coventry. They were looked after by Quaker conscientious objectors, who would not fight. This was counted as 'war work'. It was very hard. Cooking was done in an outhouse, later a chicken house. I don't know how they managed for clothes washing and baths etc.

A few of the delicate children were squeezed somehow into the house. Nanny was extra busy, helped by an adult evacuee, Mrs Haddrill, who nobody wanted because she had baby Derek with her. Uncle Lloyd scooped them up as they waited, unclaimed, at the end of a day. She became a family friend, staying until 1949. One little boy, who kept trying to escape, was tied by a rope to the nursery table at times. He and I were roped together and sent out to play, so that he couldn't run away. Nanny was an anchor for all of us. She deserves a book on her own.

In addition to her normal 'nanny duties', she used to fetch me home from school driving Mary's pony, Fanny, harnessed to a small governess cart. Our knees were wedged up against a big metal bin, in which she collected scraps for the pigs as we came home through West Buckland. She liked to gossip too. My school uniform absorbed some interesting odours. I think the people at school were by turns amused and aghast at our farm life. Messages would come through the school, "Tell Philippa not to go through Mr Skeggs' field; he has put the bull in it."

Aunty G was so busy that she sometimes forgot to be cross with me and was nice. Once she and Uncle Lloyd arrived at school and took me out for the day. Uncle Lloyd had business on Exmoor. We picnicked on Dunkery Beacon. She loved children. Quite often she was very fair. But why would she not let me join the Guides, which were run by Uncle Lloyd's unmarried sister, lovely Aunt Dot? The others all went: Mary, Penelope and the three evacuee sisters: Jean, Barbara and Grace. I have no idea. Perhaps she knew that my mother worried. The other mystery was, when I asked Aunty G for piano lessons, a harmless request as there were two pianos and Penelope was learning, the rather abrupt reply was, "Your mother said you were not to have music lessons." It was yet another restriction.

And, why did she insist on reading every one of my weekly duty letters to India, when I became old enough to write? I deeply resented this. It felt like being spied on. I couldn't say anything personal. I would have asked why they had left me behind. Had my parents told her to act as a gaoler? Children imagine strange things. It must have been just me that felt like this towards her. Uncle Lloyd, her children and, later, her grandchildren all adored her. She had a laugh like the bells of heaven.

Mary, and then Penelope, followed Angela to the Quaker boarding school in York – The Mount. This left me the only family child eating tea with Uncle Lloyd and Aunty G. I only spoke when I was spoken to. What a pain I must have been. I didn't think of myself as really family – just someone left behind.

My place, as I saw it, was on the side-lines, overawed by these very good-looking, clever, competitive cousins. My role was to love, admire and support them from the edge. They were kind to me. Angela was the most even-tempered person ever. David was a handsome dashing young man. Mary, with her mother's lovely green eyes and black hair, was the perfect elder sister, who taught me to knit. Penelope made my exclusion from Guides matter less by coming home and teaching me the things they had learned there such as semaphore. The three evacuee girls, whose lives were so different from ours, mattered as individuals. All the evacuees taught us a great deal. When they came, the Beano, the Dandy, and Radio Fun entered our lives, to add to the intake of the News Chronicle, Picture Post, The Times, and Punch. When there was really nasty news, Aunty G hid the newspapers from us.

I worshipped Uncle Lloyd. I longed to sit on his knee. I loved his tall stories. When he dragged us all out on wet Sunday afternoons to go squelching through the mud to cut logs in the wood, I only minded the cold and the wet – not him. On shooting expeditions, I trotted faithfully behind him with the retrievers, carrying dead rabbits or pheasants. He was a county councillor, an alderman, an OBE and served on umpteen committees. He was my rock. He never said a cross word to me in his life.

It was a very full childhood and, despite the undertow of my own sadness, Gerbestone was an amazing place for us all. I am very, very grateful to Uncle Lloyd and Aunty G for all they were and for all they did. At the end of their lives, I was pleased and proud to be a bit of help. I drove Aunty G to W.I. events and was on the rota David drew up for carers for Uncle Lloyd in his very old age. He lived to be 98. The day before he died, there were 16 of us quietly sitting in his bedroom.

After the War It was 1945, V E Day. When the news came over the wireless I was washing up at the kitchen sink. To celebrate the end of the wartime blackout, Uncle Lloyd set fire to a mouldy old hay rick. It burned well into the night.

Out of the blue, with a tiny bit of warning, my parents reappeared. I had stopped thinking of them much, realising I had forgotten what they looked like, though the letters kept coming and the sweets and tea at Christmas. Once Mummy sent me a red silk dress with elephants on it. She sent Mary, Penelope and me different coloured waistcoats she had knitted for us which was nice. When their car crunched up the drive, I hid in the bathroom. Here they were, with a pale freckled seven-year old boy, my brother Andrew.

We went to house sit at Croxhall on the other side of Wellington. It was the home of Uncle Tom and Aunt Alix, my mother's brother and his wife. We at Gerbestone had seen very little of them because of the war. My mother was soon in hospital. They had sailed home in rather poor conditions in a troopship designed for 500 people which was made to hold 1,500 returnees. Optimistically, my father thought I, aged 13, could cook for him, Andrew and me on a primus stove - the Aga having been let out for the summer. This of course failed. Within a day, after porridge and burnt bacon and not much else, we went and fetched Aunty Cath, my father's favourite sister, from Taunton station. She restored order. I warmed immediately to her soft Scots accent and her gurgly laugh. Thereafter we often went to stay with her in her old cottage in Suffolk. She had a barn where she painted in oils. She made the most wonderful gingerbread. During World War One she had been a VAD in charge of troop trains full of the wounded.

Then we went to stay with Granny. She had bought a four bedroom red brick villa, Grangemount, in Wellington. Life with this new mother had its moments. I was rather fat which she commented on: "Twice round the gasworks, once round Philippa". Not funny. One time, when we went shopping in Granny's car, she stopped outside a shoe shop, handed me a one-pound note and told me to go and buy myself a pair of rubber boots. In the shop there was a sturdy farm-type pair of gum boots like the ones we had at Gerbestone, for £1, so I handed over the note and took the boots out to her by the car. She told me off for wasting money, she had meant polite town type boots at half the price. However, when I said I'd take them in and explain I'd made a mistake, she wouldn't allow it. Perhaps she didn't like losing face, I don't know. I felt guilty of extravagance. There was this gulf between us.

We did come together packing a trunk with new school uniform clothes for me for Sherborne School for Girls, her old school, I liked that. We put in a green overall called a 'djibbah', green blouses, white blouses for Sunday, a brown tweed suit for

Sunday best, six pairs of vests, socks, etc., a blue and green
house tie. It made me love Sherborne even before I got there.
My parents went back to India leaving both Andrew and me at
Gerbestone.

In 1947 they had another leave. This time Daddy drove us on a
car journey up to Thurso in Caithness, his home town, visiting
family and old friends en route. The closer we got to Thurso, the
more he mellowed. It was a good holiday though nice to get back
to school after it.

Just before our sixth form exams, my parents cabled that after
that term I was to go to domestic science college, Atholl
Crescent, in Edinburgh. I burst into tears. As Angela, David, Mary
and Penelope had all gone to Oxbridge, I had set my heart on
going too. Surprisingly backing me up, Aunty G cabled a request
for this. The reply came: I could, if I won a scholarship. I worked
hard for the Higher School Certificate, in English, Latin and
French main and Spanish subsidiary, and won a State
Scholarship.

My reluctant parents therefore allowed me to stay on at school
to take the entrance exams for St Anne's Oxford to read French. I
passed, went for interview, was bowled over by Oxford itself and
was awarded a place. Much later I learned that my parents had
already paid a term's fees for Atholl Crescent. Aunty G didn't
know that at the time, nor did I. So, these fees were forfeit; also,
they were faced with two more terms of school fees, and three
years of helping supplement my scholarship; up to four years
before I would start to earn. They had not reckoned on this. It all
came out later. To them it was just proof of my disregard for

their wishes and their money. I didn't know what their wishes were.

They didn't know what my wishes were. My hope was to work hard for a First, apply for the Foreign Office, have a good career and prove to everyone that I was worth something.

By now it was 1949, two years after the partition of India. There had been much slaughter – though not in the south – and expats leaving. My mother, who had not liked India and had never been very happy there, had had two heart attacks, so my father at 57 gave up the job he loved to bring her home and hoped that reuniting the family, which they both desperately wanted, would help her. In true family style, the prospect of their returning at any time had never, ever been talked about to me or mentioned in letters till two months before it happened so what I felt was mild panic, not a daughterly rush of love and joy. They arrived - a lady with white hair and a stern-faced gentleman in plus fours with a nice laugh. I looked for the Mummy I had loved and couldn't see her. These were my parents who, after a night at Gerbestone, were to take me to live with them. To tell the truth, I felt all the excitement of getting into a cold bath. They had walked out on me.

The day we left, Aunty G said two things. One was meant to be a friendly warning; "It won't be easy." I could already see that. The other just about put the seal on a difficult relationship: "I'm glad you're going. You've caused me more worry than all the rest put together."

Thank you, Aunty G, I've tried to keep out of your way and not be a nuisance, I know I was dumped on you.

"Fortune favours the prepared mind" (Pasteur). My mind was all prepared to explore the world, form opinions, on my own as I thought. I didn't know my parents were intending to come back and reclaim me. I thought they had abandoned me to Aunty G and would stay in India. I didn't grudge it. If they could have a nice time without me, fine, I would manage somehow without them. But here they were. Oh help.

Mount Pleasant Farm

We went to a delightful four-bedroom house, Mount Pleasant Farm, on the edge of Sampford Peverell, a village on the Somerset-Devon border near Tiverton. Everything my parents brought home: solid Indian rosewood furniture and thick Indian wool carpets, fitted exactly, carefully planned. The previous tenants, Mr and Mrs Pocock, friends of my parents, had left a list of people in the village to 'know' and not to 'know' – oh dear. I was to cook for £1 a week. I had picked it up from watching Norah in the Gerbestone kitchen. Aunty G must have said it would be all right. I was deeply proud of this. They were both tired and not at all well. They needed time to adjust to retirement, to English cold, to austerity Britain.

My father had worked as tea estate manager and group manager for Brooke Bond and latterly was in the Madras Legislative Assembly which sounded quite grand. With transition into retirement he was bored. As he was an outdoor person, he soon found golfing friends, or people to go shooting or fishing with, including Uncle Lloyd. Later he was a special constable. He made efforts in the garden. My mother said he didn't know the difference between a plant and a weed. He knew about radishes. No radish reached the kitchen because he ate them all.

In India my mother had lived in the gilded cage of a memsahib, mostly alone in the bungalow, no nearby shops, family or neighbours to meet; keeping track of household spending, giving orders, filling her days with letter writing and knitting; feeling the heat. Cooks did the cooking. Ayah looked after first me, later, Andrew. The gardener gardened. There was social life at The Club once or twice a week in the evenings, where tea planters met colleagues over (several) drinks, members played tennis and bridge and danced. Sometimes there were children's parties. Wives flirted with and kept their eyes on husbands, not always their own. My mother said Daddy was "the most popular man in the district." He kept clear of entanglements.

Back in England it was much better for her, there were shops in the village, family at the end of the telephone, she could do some gardening, have her hair done in Tiverton, buy clothes. She supervised the cleaning lady and me. She could take the car over to Wellington to visit relatives, or to Taunton for shopping. A nice family of retired tea planters were within visiting distance, they compared notes. There was a little coterie of retired people in the village. My godfather and his wife came to stay. My mother knitted socks for my father, lovely jumpers for me and Andrew. She joined the W.I. Her one luxury was a monthly antiques magazine. They took a newspaper which my father had to have first.

I hoped they would start off by saying "Sorry we left you". I think their showering me with clothes etc. was an attempt to "make it up" to me as Aunt Alix thought, but it needed saying, then I would have loved to begin to trust them, forgive them and start to accept them back into my life as parents. In an attempt to get this put straight, I tried to explain to Mummy how shattering it was to find they had simply gone, but I couldn't find the words, I burst into tears and she jumped on me. "You were five. You were old enough to understand. You are wallowing in self-pity." This took my breath away. She just didn't get it. She followed up with "You don't know all the disappointments I've had". No, at the time I didn't. Although it wasn't a very motherly thing to say just then, when years later I understood a little of what she had gone through, it made more sense. I am so sorry. I could have started by saying how much I missed her.

How, one may ask, can anyone of any age understand why a sudden departure is not announced? Surely this is an omission of a common courtesy? I wrestled then and forever after with the question of forgiveness. Surely it should be unconditional. When one person, who has omitted a courtesy, thinks firmly they have done the right thing, how is the second person, who feels hurt, supposed to proceed? On what basis is the relationship, if there is one, to continue or to be mended? If the first person insists the second is being unreasonable, what then? It becomes complicated.

I think that she and my father thought they had given me – their sacrifice for sure – a perfect childhood and I wasn't living up to their expectations or being grateful. Looking back, this is true, I don't remember saying thank you. I was full of fear. This is my best shot at explaining the truly awful six months that followed. It was a cat's cradle of misunderstanding on both sides.

I felt them scrutinising me all day as I worked. The first week, they told me, "If you do something right, we won't say anything. If you do something wrong, we will tell you." This was ominous. I don't think this strategy would be found in any modern textbook on child rearing or personnel management. In six months I didn't once hear the words "thank you" or "well done" which would have meant a lot. I found myself remembering how Aunty G, who was so often cross with me, never failed to say thank you when, for instance, someone fetched her a cup of tea. One felt appreciated. It was the Reverend Sidney Smith, I believe, who said "Praise is the best diet for us." Opposed to that was the Victorian "spare the rod and spoil the child".

I had gained confidence at school. I was an early school prefect, head of house for two terms, I was one of three who won State scholarships, giving the whole school a day off. In the family I still felt rejected and unconfident. As I had not prevailed on my mother to understand how I hadn't coped, I gave up again, remained silent and confused which they, obviously, found infuriating. I accuse myself of laziness.

A few phrases from Wild Goose of Iona describe the impasse:

Where family life has lost its bliss and silences endorse mistrust
or anger boils and tempers flare as love comes under
threat....where people cannot take the strain... what pattern will
the future weave ?

They gave me the second-best bedroom with my own antique desk, and rosewood bookcases they had had specially made. Mummy who loved clothes more than I ever would, bought me a red suit, a green suit, two blue summer dresses, a winter coat, a heavy fur coat (what a bone of contention that became), a ball gown, high heeled shoes, custom made shoes (worn once, they hurt), and an outfit to be presented in which took several fittings to make.

They took Penelope and me to Buckingham Palace to be presented. Dressed in our finery, we walked up wide red carpeted stairs, stood for ages three deep on either side of a red carpeted passage. I saw the heads of King George and Queen Elizabeth and Princess Margaret's white hat over someone's shoulder as the royals passed. We waited there some more hearing faint voices from the great room where the action was, before following the throng of smartly dressed strangers down other stairs to eat crustless cucumber sandwiches off bone china in a marquee. My feet! I never wore those white shoes again. My father hired a suit from Moss Bros. It was a bit tight. We rode in taxis, we stayed in a hotel. Apparently, you couldn't have tea with a rajah if you hadn't been presented. If any rajah would like to invite me, please get in touch, then all will not have been in vain.

These were people who thought I was extravagant. It was like the old joke about declining a verb, "I am generous. You are extravagant. He/she is a spendthrift."

Being 'grown up' seemed to be all clothes, shoes, hats and tea parties. At tea parties my mother talked non-stop about Andrew with me sitting there. Andrew told me it was the same with him; she talked heaps about me with him just sitting there. Again, I was thankful for Aunty G's lack of gossip. Although 'comparisons are odious' I found myself hankering for the freedoms of

Gerbestone while feeling this was disloyal. All this churned round inside me.

Unwittingly, I shocked them. Using their new, generous dress allowance, wanting to keep warm, I bought a pair of dark red velvet corduroy trousers. Why not? Aunty G wore dungarees. Women in factories wore trousers. However, my parents remembered 1920's England. They hadn't seen wartime clothes. As I walked down to the village wearing the trousers, my father followed me slowly in the family car with the window open shouting "Philip! Philip!". I wasn't their biddable five-year old any more. I was slipping out of their grasp. I wasn't doing it to be annoying, I was busy being eighteen. I didn't drink, smoke, or watch out for boys, I worked and worried about my untouched Oxford reading list. I shocked them by wanting to help the neighbour farmer with haymaking. This was frowned on as unladylike. To me it was normal, it was what happened on a farm, everyone pitched in. When I talked about Gerbestone, my mother froze. I did so want to share all the beauty and fun of it with her.

I shocked them again by saying I might hitchhike somewhere. Many of my generation did. Father said he would beat me if I did. This shocked me. If he had beaten me I would have left. I did hitch hike, I didn't tell him. (How to turn an obedient person into a rebel?). I started telling him he was ordering me about like a coolie. It began to feel as if I was guilty whatever I did.

Several times he said to me "What do you want to do?" I didn't really know, I would have welcomed some ideas. My suggestion of journalism received the thumbs down. I choked back the words "Get away from you." Although work options for girls were on the increase, the conventional ones were still teaching, nursing, secretarial, or social work. He wanted me to stand on my own feet, to work. I was always very grateful for this. He knew how Mummy had had to be a stay-at-hometill-married-or-not daughter, as Granny had refused to let her study medicine, even though in the family cousin Cecilia Fox, the same age as my mother, was an early woman medical student at the Bristol Royal infirmary.

They had punctual well-cooked meals, breakfast at eight, lunch at one, afternoon tea around four, (at tea parties, everything was home cooked), supper at six thirty, put in front of them for the six months between us moving in and the start of the October university term. There was no complaint about my cooking. I did overhear my mother telling someone how she missed being brought early morning tea, my father had to do it. However, they usually chose meal times (when Andrew was away at prep school) to announce my failings. I was glad when Andrew was at home because they didn't do it in front of him. As more faults I was unaware of were added I became more nervous. My manners were bad. I was "house devil, street angel". I thought this was going it a bit; I tried to be polite to the respectable people who met in each others' 26 houses for sherry after church. The poor vicar was not considered acceptable and never invited. I felt so sorry for him and his librarian wife.

With Aunty G I had tried to be quiet and unobtrusive but it was a much smaller house than Gerbestone. The pressure was on to be like them, there didn't seem to be any space to be me. It was as if the twelve years of their absence, two-thirds of my life, didn't count. I wanted to prattle on about those years, to include them in what we had been doing and learning. My mother didn't seem to want to hear. I should have gone on regardless perhaps. I was a "wet". Daddy woke me one June morning - I had tried to sleep out and retreated to the dining room floor when it rained - to announce without preamble "Your mother is heart-broken over you". What had I done? My mother said disapprovingly "All a man wants is peace". So did I. Some more of his views were: "You are a great disappointment to me" (this was after I had cooked for, and washed up after, a tea party and, very tired, went to sit for a few minutes beside him in the garden. It really hurt). "You don't know the price of margarine." (They didn't teach margarine at Sherborne, only how to make eclairs). "I don't want a blue stocking daughter". "Girls of your age are earning a living". These came from his deep disapproval of my place at Oxford. It had been all right for the Gerbestone girls he so much admired, but not for me.

One early morning, when my mother's voice was going up and down – I could hear it in my bedroom through open windows - I crept into Andrew's small room next theirs and put a glass to the wall to listen in. Sure enough, it was about me. "... but G says she is extremely thrifty..." It was nice to know Aunty G was defending me. It confirmed my suspicions that my mother discussed my failings around the family. There was ample proof of this later. I beat a hasty retreat.

"How lovely to have a grown-up daughter". I didn't feel like one. Unfortunately, all the years of not knowing they would ever return had dimmed, for me, the memory of joyous family unity. There was the fur coat episode. Mummy took me to a fur coat shop in Taunton. I sat watching her looking at herself in full length mirrors trying on different fur coats. She asked for my opinion of one, a "beaver lamb". Not very interested, I said "It looks very nice." Back at the house she presented it to me. "I bought this for you." When I was five she had dressed me in the sweetest little fur coat, I loved it. That was then.

I ask myself, was I tactless, or honest, or what? My response was not," Oh thank you how kind". It was "I don't want a fur coat. You tried it on for yourself. Take it back." She wouldn't. First, I was furious at not having been allowed to try it on, if it was for me. I could have saved her the money, all I wanted was a duffle coat. Second, I didn't want it on principle; it probably cost the equivalent of a half a farm worker's yearly wages; making friends with evacuees had opened my eyes a little. Third, it was horrible, heavy and stiff. (I endured it, once, on a freezing day at a wedding in Exford). Fourth, I wasn't really into clothes, they were what you put on in the morning. I wanted them simple and suitable. How could anyone wear a fur coat on a bicycle going to lectures? She was mortally offended, to her it was the height of luxury. For her generation and social class, it was. Both Aunty G and Mary had beaver lamb coats.

Poor Mummy, wanting to have a little girl to dress all those years.

Daddy tried to show me things too. He took me to an otter hunt. I can still hear the poor creature's screams. He took me to a boxing match which my memory refuses to register. He tried and failed to teach me to shoot and to play golf. My driving lessons with him were abandoned after the car scraped the vicar's gatepost. I was scared of this strange man.

They tried so hard. She said to someone "We tried everything". It could be said, everything except patience and a little encouragement; relationships take time. They didn't know why I didn't yet trust them. She hadn't listened. They so regretted the lost years. I still feel guilty. I didn't know where to start. With hindsight, I should have given up Oxford, got a job in Tiverton in the library or a veg shop, found digs with someone in the church congregation, and gone home on the bus at weekends to help with ironing, and generally try to be nicer to my mother, so that we could get to know each other gradually. It would have been nice to feel I had a mother, one who would listen. Not having got used to her while growing up, I didn't understand her. It was all too much.

Aunty G and Uncle Lloyd's liberal views had formed my approach to life, and suddenly I was supposed to think and behave as my parents expected. My father flatly refused to sign a form for me to go on the parish register because I said I'd vote Labour (partly to annoy him). Aunty G was a feminist even before the term was common; in my parents' house everything revolved around the man. Subtle differences but important. My mother had fitted herself neatly into the role of dutiful wife; why was I bent on annoying them by wearing trousers, buying a radio, enjoying Shakespeare, and presuming on more education than they thought fit for a girl? (When it was Andrew's turn, they sent him to Cambridge). If I had known I was walking into all this perhaps I might have been more circumspect. Perhaps not.

It is possible they saw me as an off-the-peg ready-made adult, which I'm afraid I wasn't. I do wonder if my mother's selfesteem was seriously low after all those lonely years, missing England.

As I was leaving for Oxford, Mummy offered this: "If you had been a servant, we would have sacked you. You need to see a psychiatrist." Too late, an equally unkind retort came to mind: "If you had been my employers, I would have quit."

As soon as possible I went to the St Anne's college GP to ask for a referral.

"My parents are just back from India, we aren't getting on."

"Of course I will refer you. Tell your parents they must come too."

I wrote to tell them this. They did not mention it again. What a shame. I had hoped that an impartial skilled outside person might be able to help us understand one another.

To be in Oxford was wonderful, I am only sorry I was in such an interior mess, I did not thrive. My tutor Annie Barnes despaired of me until she had my parents and me to Sunday sherry in my third year. Afterwards she arranged for me to stay up so as to read in peace during the last vacation before Schools. I scraped a Third. Hopes of a First were gone. After, I had recurring nightmares about never finding the library and arriving for Schools wearing my pyjamas, having not studied at all.

To London

After Oxford they told me they were sending me to London to do a secretarial course. Penelope had done a short one in Oxford. Although I wasn't keen, what was there to do? I begged with tears for Exeter, because from there I could visit on the bus at weekends, for us all to get to know each other better. Living near, but not on top of each other. London - which I loathed - was too far. Mummy said "We've already paid. You aren't going to waste our money again like you did the last time, are you?". She was referring to cancelling Atholl Crescent. Had Aunty G and I known it was prepaid, of course it would have made a difference.

I went to London on the train with two suitcases.

Instead of the lodgings they had booked for me (oh dear) I stayed with Monica and Arthur, the parents of my school friend Jean in Thames Ditton. It was a haven of fun, intelligent conversation, purposeful living and kindness. They were darlings. They kept their doors open to me for the rest of their lives. Jean is still a good friend, her elder son James is my godson.

After doing as much of the course as I could bear, with occasional days playing hooky on Hampstead Heath, I got a job typing invoices mostly, in the accounts department at Victor Gollancz the publishers in Covent Garden for £6.10.0d a week, and a room at the YWCA opposite the British Museum. Soon Ann from Oxford invited me to share her flat in Kensington, plus another friend, Anne from the youth group which we belonged to at St Mary Abbot's Kensington run by the curate John Habgood (later Archbishop of York). God was trying to make me aware of His presence. I had said to myself, if my parents represented Christianity in the C of E, there must be something better. However, I had had the lovely example of Granny which drew me back.

London was better than expected though I was homesick for the slower pace of the West Country, for green fields, for knowing there were family members around (Granny died when I was 16). I wrote some really angry letters to my mother which I deeply regret. My state of mind was very odd. I wrongly saw being sent to London as a banishment for not being the right kind of daughter. At work, in every one of the 22 jobs I ever had (counting even the smallest) I set aside my private life but it was still there at the end of the day to swallow me up. Weighed down by family disapproval, with all their comments rattling in my mind, I felt I was a nonperson, powerless and not part of the family. I was in the shallow end of paranoia, trying to keep socially afloat, telling myself all the time I'd got it wrong, and must try harder. It was a sort of perverse loyalty. Now, it is all a blur.

I didn't go home for Christmas or holidays for four years. When I did, my parents were shocked at how thin I was. They generously paid for me to stay six weeks with some people they had stayed with near Marbella - then just a few bungalows - in south Spain. The host and hostess were fun. I slept for 14 hours a night and put on a stone in weight. After, in gratitude I went down to Devon for a week to see my parents. Back in London a letter from my mother arrived with another complaint. Oh no not again.

My friend Jean was so happy in Canada, she came to England once a year bubbling over with how good it was. I took due notice.

Uncle Lloyd came up to town on business. He took me out to supper and a musical (he went to sleep) and came back to see Ann's flat. He asked me to "be nice to" my parents. My conscience smote me. There was still a terrible muddle in my head. My mother came up to town and took me to a play. She wouldn't come back to see the flat. My father wrote and offered to take me out for a meal so we could "tell each other why we don't get on". Although it was an olive branch, I remembered how my mother wouldn't listen and all the mealtime complaints, two against one, and said No. It could have begun a reconciliation. I think my not going back had hit them. My father was a very decent man. This was the first of three things I might have said Yes to. What a difference it would have made.

The other two things were a job offer and a proposal of marriage.

The job offer came out of the blue from Kenneth Hyde, a minor actor and sought-after script writer. He sent Jean, his new, second, wife, out to work because she was a distraction, and used her wages to pay me to type his scripts. I couldn't help butting in all the time with my bright ideas, which he surprisingly liked. It was sheer joy to go to work every day and love it. Once or twice we went down to Shepherd's Bush where he was playing Machiavelli in a film being shot there. It was lovely chaos. A girl I had been at school with was working in a caravan as secretary to an actor who was playing Robin Hood on another film set; she was answering his sacksful of fan mail. Lesser known actors were wandering around in stages of undress. Edmund Purdom was a sight for sore eyes in a string vest. Kenneth, made up and sweating dreadfully in a full length quasi-mediaeval purple velvet robe would come into his dressing room between takes, and together we would thrash out another scene of an A J Cronin novel he was turning into a screen play.

One day he offered me a partnership in their three-man script writing syndicate. What an honour.

The suggestion of marriage came from Peter. We had each gone, on our own, to a Prom at the Albert Hall, leaving our Lambrettas in the designated space. There were some lovely Mozart serenades that evening. I sat soaking up the music in the top gallery (near the gents, the door kept banging). The air was warm and balmy in the late evening. I said hello to the person whose Lambretta was next to mine. He said something in reply, we went somewhere for a coffee. Thereafter we met now and then for coffee or baked beans in my room (Ann having got married and needing her flat). Peter worked in an office. He was a Presbyterian who taught Sunday school. He even came down with me to Devon for some fresh air and survived meeting my parents. He was a good friend, we hadn't even held hands. I asked Mummy if she liked him. She sniffed. "He's Jewish." (He had a Jewish surname). Oh dear. One evening, sitting on the very small rented sofa he said quietly "I'd like to marry you." "Oh Peter, I've just bought a ticket on a boat to Canada."

I had never thought of me and marriage, that was for all my beautiful cousins, not me. Also, I was afraid to invite him into such a family mess. On the contrary he would, I am now sure, have defended me where needed, called me to account when I was out of order, and been a loyal, faithful partner and friend. So sorry, Peter, wherever you are I hope you have had a long, happy, fulfilled life.

There were three golden chances to get my life on track. Winston Churchill said "When people trip over the truth, they pick themselves up and rush away in the opposite direction" (or some such remark). That was me, I didn't recognise chances of happiness even when handed to me on a plate.

A couple of weeks before these two offers I had bought a ticket on a Cunard liner called the Ivernia to go to Jean in Canada.

In my cabin there was a tear stained letter from my mother with a little carefully wrapped packet of primroses. It was tangible, small, it looked like real love. The person I am now might have caught the next boat back and moved heaven and earth to get things put right.

The voyage took five days. We were eight single girls, emigrating for work. They put us on a round table for meals. We had the same waiter every day. We teased him rotten. He loved it. On the voyage I read The Lord of The Rings, just out; I found myself shouting at a South African about the apartheid situation. I prayed for Nelson Mandela for years. A pair of girls called Thelma and Doris asked me to join them sharing a flat in Montreal, the boat's first port of call. A fourth cousin on the Fox side met me in his VW beetle, was very good to me, showed me the city and took me out to dinner. Everything was big, the limousines, the portions on plates, even the robins. While we were eating, his car was broken into, my suitcase with my very early edition of The Lord of the Rings, was stolen. Hello Canada.

Canada

In 1959, my second year there, word came that my mother had inoperable secondary brain cancer. Six months earlier she had begun getting breakfast for Daddy and Andrew at 2 a.m. Other odd things happened. The first guess was senile dementia. She was 59. Tests revealed the real reason for increasingly strange behaviour. I flew home, worried that she was in great pain. She wasn't. She greeted me "Hello darling" then talked of people dead for many years as if they were still alive.

It was a small funeral on a wintry day. We buried her ashes in the family plot at Rockwell Green cemetery on the edge of Wellington, alongside her parents. May she rest in peace and rise in glory, and God will wipe all tears from her eyes.

I was in trouble again. Aunty G berated me for not comforting my father. I tried to say something and got it wrong. I didn't feel anything and was ashamed. There was this great gulf between us. I had nothing to keep me in Canada and had we had a normal loving family life, I would have chucked in my job in a typing pool and gone home to live with my father and work in Tiverton. After all the things he had said, which had put such doubts in me, I thought I wouldn't be welcome or useful. I felt so sad about this. Aunty G didn't know the half of it.

The whole story of our family is of people being too knotted up to speak.

I went to stay with Penelope. In the car with her on the Exeter by-pass I managed to blurt out with tears the way my parents had left me (this was a first). Word spread through that family. It was a total surprise. "Oh, how cruel" from Aunty G "we all thought you knew." She changed. She was friendly after that and Penelope told me she didn't like to be reminded of her strictness.

Now that he was on his own, Daddy came out to visit. He had been the happy-go-lucky youngest of a large family in Thurso near John O' Groats; three brothers had emigrated to Canada. The widow of Will, the eldest, Aunt Madie, had no children. She was really happy to have a niece nearby. Visiting my parents in England she had been very taken with my father; now she asked him and me to stay, and Uncle Har (Harold) an ex rancher from Calgary, stayed too. It was a rather splendid reunion for them.

Daddy took the sight-seeing cross-Canada train to visit Uncle Jim in Vancouver. Jim had never had any help for his shell shock from World War One. People were supposed to get over it. Daddy said, "He went to war a laughing boy; he came out a wizened old man". He had endured the whole war without a scratch. Daddy had survived emotionally intact, as far as one could see. It was perhaps a blessing, a mixed one, that he was gassed and shot in the jaw during the fighting on the Somme. He spent the next two years in hospital in Somerville College, Oxford. I met Uncle Jim later.

Canada was good for me. I visited Jean and her family often, joined an active young church group, began to play reasonable tennis in long hours of lovely warm weather, made some lovely lifelong friends. There was a feeling of freedom, a 'can do' attitude without class hang-ups. And no family to keep on telling me off. Wonderful.

My first job in Toronto was in the typing pool at the Electric Reduction Co. of Canada Ltd., a branch of Albright & Wilson in England, manufacturers of agricultural chemicals (I wasn't as pro-organic then as now). At interview they asked, did I know anyone at head office? Yes, Mr. Topley, father of my friend Ann in London I said naively. He was only the CEO.

After about a year they promoted me to be secretary to the Company Secretary. For some reason he wasn't too happy and eventually smoked himself to death with cigarettes, cigars and a pipe or two every day. As I survived the job, the smoke, and doing the payroll manually for 140 employees every month, when he died they wanted to give me the job. Having no training in accounting and company law, I demurred.

While I was hesitating, I attended a conference on journalism. This would have been my second choice after the Foreign Office had my parents not returned. I asked a question, giving my name and occupation. At the end, a friendly young man spoke to me. Would I like to work for him?

He was Dr John T Saywell, Professor of Modern Canadian History at the University of Toronto, a TV star, often seen on the evening news talking about Canadian politics; editor of the Canadian Annual Review, etc.

My father's prejudice against blue stocking academics was far off the mark with the University of Toronto History guys. Away from the work they were very good at, they were as funny as they come. Maurice Careless when he became Head of Department assured them that he was a step in the right direction, his predecessor's name having been Professor Wrong. One of the professors was proverbially absent minded. He owned and rented out about five houses; legend had it that he just kept on forgetting and buying another one. One day he mistook a colleague's identical office for his and sat down at 'his' desk. When the rightful occupant arrived, he said "Yes Archie, what can I do for you?

" Jack and Pat Saywell often asked me to babysit their three very bright kids, and we became good friends. He had a wonderful collection of modern Canadian art.

Soon he was appointed Dean of the Faculty at the fledgling York University. His job was to recruit the brightest and best to help it grow. They wanted him so much, he bargained to take his research assistant (me), so he had two offices on the go and three secretaries. It was starting small – it soon outgrew the lovely place where we worked, Glendon Hall, set in large lovely gardens; there were five student residences for 150 girls and boys, offices, dining and lecture halls in the extensive grounds.

The next year, they appointed me 'don' in one of the three girls' residences, because I had an Oxford degree. The other four dons were lecturers. We ate in hall. It was a short walk across campus around the goldfish ponds and between the huge trees to my office. We were allowed to use the swimming pool and the tennis courts. I had landed on my feet.

Student problems in those days were few; health worries, exam anxiety, homesickness, a bit of loneliness, sometimes a slip up with alcohol, some hilarious practical jokes. Don Rickerd, the college Registrar, was in overall charge of the students. They adored him. He had a light touch. One morning he woke to see his VW Beetle placed in a ring of yew trees, whose trunks were close together at ground level then leaned out. He remarked mildly to someone that he had to go downtown at lunchtime for a meeting. The VW reappeared on the road.

On weekends I found time to do two translations from French into English for Ryerson's. It was good to make use of my degree. The second one I really liked, it was Folk Tales of Canada, one from each of the ten provinces.

The Assistant Dean was Edward Patullo, a quiet friendly man seconded from Harvard. It was out of character for him to come in after lunch and aim a savage kick at the metal filing cabinet in my office.

President Kennedy had been shot in Dallas.

While I was in residence at York I met a Scottish paediatrician, Dr Bill D., who was re-qualifying at the Sick Children's Hospital. I don't want to write much about it. He had just renounced his love, Pat, because he thought he was too old for her (7 years). She married someone else, had two girls with him, got divorced, and eventually re-met and married Bill. They are still together in 2018. I wasn't the answer to his dilemma, nor he to mine.

Compared to what he saw every day, he thought we at York had a cushioned life. He liked the swimming. I got pregnant in June

1965. I did not see him again. I did not want an abortion, I decided at once on adoption so that he/she could have two parents, a settled home, love and security. I had no family nearby.

That August my father invited me to go with him, Uncle Lloyd and Aunty G on holiday to Thurso, his home town not far from John 'O Groats. He drove us up in his car. We had a leisurely journey, doing some sightseeing on the Borders including Abbotsford, Sir Walter Scott's house.

We had a good time. Uncle Lloyd and my father fished (fish not biting much), Aunty G and I explored and joined them at lunchtime with hotel sandwiches. They stayed in the Ormlie Lodge Hotel not far from Viewfirth, my dad's large boyhood home, which had become the club for workers at the nuclear power plant Dounreay. The local joke about Dounreay was that it could power one light bulb. He and I stayed with Mrs Lyall a family friend.

Daddy saw me off on the early train at the halt outside town. The station lady came out in slippers and dressing gown waving a flag. I think she knew the driver. It was the last time I saw my father, I couldn't bear to tell him my news.

Back to Canada to face the music.

I left York University. I worked as a temp, staying first with the Saywells then with Viv James, secretary in Biology at York. She and her charming mother were so kind. Jamaicans are so matter of fact. Catherine Mary was born at 9 am on Sunday 6th March

1966. It was a horrible week. The charge nurse came and drank tea with me in the middle of my sleepless nights.

On Friday March 11th I formally handed her over in her shawl, on the hospital steps, to the representative of the adopting couple. It was a cold grey day, gritty old snow on the roads. With her, I gave an inherited gold filigree Maltese cross. I wanted her to know she was loved. Silently, I gave her to God.

Bruce Lawson fetched me to his and Mary's house in Rosedale. They dragged me to a party that night. I found myself listening to a complete stranger. She was distraught; she had had an abortion.

I do not recommend giving away a baby. I could not look at little girls for thirty years.

I had to go for 'counselling' to the adoption agency - the Childrens' Aid. The lady volunteer was a doctor's wife who wore orthopaedic brown leather shoes and was no help at all.

The week after signing the final adoption papers in that office, news came that my father had died suddenly after a heart attack. He was on holiday in the Canaries with his friend George 'Hunter' Waters, his great pal, another retired tea planter from Thurso. He felt ill and went home to Andrew and Hermione in Wellington. I had a premonition. The day before I rang Uncle Lloyd who said he seemed fine. It was good that we had had that time in Scotland.

I drove out to Banff in my VW Beetle. Prairies are lovely with the mist rising at five in the morning. I stayed up the hill with Drs Ian and Priscilla Wilson. She was Penelope's school friend. He was an Irish GP and surgeon. I had a two-month holiday job selling good antiques and awful china knickknacks in an upmarket antique shop run by their friend Sheila in the High Street, to overweight retired American couples. The US grand tour included a few nights at the Banff Springs Hotel. Ian was the hotel GP. He came home each evening with fresh scurrilous or absurd anecdotes which he related over Priscilla's cordon bleu cooking. Some suppers lasted four hours. Being with people and busy was a life saver.

Life at the Wilsons' was never dull. On weekends they had all sorts of expeditions with friends, a madcap middle European doctor, Milosz, and an artist, Gordon. He made a tidy living selling his oil paintings of the Rockies or Lake Louise. Ian bounced his jokes off his straight guy, the highly amused Priscilla. A bit less funny when he didn't come home for his birthday supper. It all seemed normal. They would have been the ideal people to tell about Catherine, they wished I had. I wish I had. I was still Little Miss No Speech. When I left as they refused payment I gave them the biggest dictionary I could find, for Scrabble. Ian set out to find all the rudest words he could.

I went to see Uncle Jim in Vancouver. It took much persuasion to convince the Social Services I really was his niece. "Shell shock" was only officially recognised and given the label Post Traumatic Stress Disorder, PTSD, in 1980. He didn't marry, he had worked as an office boy, he lived in one large room. He and his friend Mary treated me royally. They showed me round Vancouver, including the spectacular Butchart Gardens. When I mentioned the Great War he paled and shook The horror of those four years were still like yesterday for him. He has a special place in my heart. What a brave, neglected hero he was. Heaven knows how many thousands are needing help today.

 Back in Toronto I trained to be a Registered Nurse in a new school for women between 30 and 50, the Quo Vadis. It was ground breaking. It was written up in the readers' digest. Miss Mackenzie, the founder, knew about Catherine. A wise person, she had nursed in India. It was mentally and physically stretching. Each one of our class had a story, including three nuns. Sister Marcella, only girl with eight brothers, surprised and alarmed the – male – consultants by marching up to them with tricky questions; Sister Lapointe drove huskies in the Arctic and set broken bones but fled from psychiatric patients; Sister Bernadetta's passion for watching ice hockey on TV got in the way of her homework. Sisters, we loved you. I did best at psychiatry, I felt right at home with them. I took a violent schizophrenic out for bat and ball practice. He did throw the ball rather hard.

After graduation, to repay my grant from Ontario, I worked a year at our training hospital. The head nurse hated Quo Vadis nurses; we were sissies who hadn't trained on nights. She refused to accept my report of how ill my patient in isolation was; so, deeply concerned, I told one of our teachers, who knew the consultant, who came … The young man walked out alive. My name was mud, the fate of whistle blowers. A nasty taste of hospital politics.

I was glad to get away to a neurosurgical ward at the Wellesley. Lots to learn. Brain problems come in all sorts of ways; the go go dancer who hit her head on the rail; the navvy who was often in on Saturdays after fist fights; the janitor who fell eighteen feet down a lift shaft; the teacher who had a benign tumour the size of a tennis ball; the junkie whose bullet whizzed between both lobes of his brain just singeing them; the little old man who went across the road in the snow wearing dressing gown and slippers to the bank to cash his only Christmas card. Sad as it often was, when someone walked out well it was all worth it. They gave me a surprisingly good report.

I wanted to go home. I was never going to see Catherine again. My brother had four small children. Aunt Alix had at last explained to me that my mother, trusting the family doctor for advice, had been told: "It's bad for children to cry. Don't say anything. Just go". Which, of course - going against nature - she did; doctors must be obeyed. In the agony of leaving, she forgot to tell Aunty G of what she was about to do. I can't help feeling that she must all along have had a deep nagging sense of guilt about it.

G, never a believer in doctors, would have ignored him. She believed in "Dr. Diet, Dr. Quiet and Dr. Merryman."

Alix also said that Lloyd and G had offered to have me, it wasn't a question of their arms being twisted as I had thought. They had a big house and big hearts.

I returned in 1970.

England

I lived and worked in Bristol. I went for weekends with my three remaining aunts, Aunty G, Aunt Alix and godmother Edna, to see Andrew and Hermione and their four children in London, various cousins, and Monica and Arthur in Hampshire. Arthur, in World War 1, had 'gone over the top' 35 times but never been hit. He never spoke of it and renounced the army. Monica had been a Guide Commissioner; she taught the local burglar's children to play the recorder. Such wonderful friends. It was good to be on home soil.

As a Canadian RN, the English system required me to retrain briefly to become State Registered. The Canadian nursing shifts were three of eight hours each, I loved the work. At the Bristol Royal Infirmary, the brutal twelve- hour night shift was too much for my weak foot. Nor was I impressed by the cockroach on my shoulder at dinner in the residence, or those in the passage under the road either. In 1971 I had to leave. I started three other jobs concurrently.

In the afternoons I was cook in Hyde lodge at St Christopher's, the Rudolf Steiner school on the Downs. I've always loved schools. A builder needed a couple of mornings' secretarial help, and on Monday mornings I typed letters for Rev Tony Baker, part time vicar (since when has any vicar been able to be part time?) of Redland Parish Church: he was also part time Director of Pastoral Studies at Trinity Theological College. This was an eye opener, I knew very little of how the church worked. Whenever he was on the phone I snatched a look at one of his many books on Pastoral Care. Life was spartan for the Bakers. Tony, uncomplaining, put up with things the next incumbent wanted changed.

It was two different kinds of hectic life: from the vicarage where there could be 36 letters to bash out on the typewriter set up on their dining table, to the hurly burly of cooking for 45. My kitchen 'assistant' Edward laid tables, helped tidy up and baked bread every day. He was a sweet 35-year-old, an ex-pupil with a reading age of 12. Cooking for 45 is like cooking for four only more so; you multiply the amounts and the time. The evening meal took four hours because in the Steiner world gadgets are verboten, no whisks, everything manual. A useful tip is, rinse the great pots at once; my first day, cleaning encrusted pans took hours.

God was moving in on me. In the mornings, honouring my Quaker upbringing, I went to Redland Quaker Meeting, conveniently two doors down from my flat; because of working for Tony, and honouring my evangelical granny, I started going to Redland's evening services. After a while I began to go to Redland all the time.

I loved the school but couldn't truthfully become a Steiner disciple (they said he wrote the Fifth Gospel). In 1974 during an appointment at the newly established Whiteladies' Health Centre, my GP, Michael Whitfield, discovered I needed a more settled existence and marched me along the corridor to the Administrator saying "Here's the secretary we've been looking for."

God got even nearer. One of the doctors and his wife asked me to tea on a Saturday. I cycled two miles, up from Redland across the Downs to their lovely house in Stoke Bishop, for four o'clock. Arriving wet and cold, looking forward to buttery crumpets, there was a shock. The house was empty. They had forgotten. This small seeming-rejection hit hard. Going back up the hill, I stopped off at St Mary's Stoke Bishop to sit in the dry for a few minutes at the back. Behind the altar was a frieze in what I think is called bas relief of the Last Supper, with Jesus in the middle, one arm raised. As I looked it seemed that Jesus' hand was reaching out to me in love, acceptance and friendship, undeserved, much needed, filling the void that nothing had filled after my parents walked away. When I later read about C.S. Lewis's conversion on the top of a Headington bus, I knew what he meant. I felt warmed all over.

Slowly, life changed. I still couldn't make sense of what had gone wrong with my parents nor how I might have put it right. I wondered if I would ever be forgiven or would people see right through me and find I was useless as they had. But it felt like going in the right direction. I told Tony Baker. He was pleased. In the church community there was love and friendliness unlike anything I had met elsewhere. The church coped with large numbers by running Home Fellowship groups of about a dozen people each. You could get to know a few people well over Bible study, discussion and coffee.

The vicar chose an agenda which he circulated, then left us to study it or something else. It became a mini family, very good for singles like me. I stayed in one for many years.

My last job in Bristol was as a secretary at Trinity Theological College. I loved it. We office staff began the day with prayers in the Bursar's office. I worked for the Director of Pastoral Studies and the Director of Mission. Among other things I had to ring up vicars and ask if they would like a 'preaching team' to come and do a practice sermon. The answer was always yes. Each year my boss did a 'job review'. Did I like the work? What could make it better? The other girls were envious.

The Principal was kindly Dr. George Carey. His in-tray was often piled six inches high. His secretary was always glad of a helping hand. He was accessible to everyone. (Heaven knows how high his pile was at Bath and Wells and later Canterbury. What a job). The students were great characters. They came from all over the world. I tried to help an Egyptian and a South Korean with their English because they hadn't got their English Proficiency Certificate. On the once-a-week French-speaking lunch table there was my friend Alphonse, who spoke four languages fluently and went on to do a D Phil at the Sorbonne before returning home. He couldn't understand Arthur Scargill not being locked up. Politics in Rwanda were so different. His lovely life ended when he was cut down on the steps of Kigali Cathedral.

Health Problems

A job I haven't mentioned was, in 1981, secretary to 68 teaching staff at Bristol Grammar School. Here my health, from good genes and a free-range farm childhood, took a beating. In my office there were: a huge photocopier used all day by the staff of upper and lower schools; an inky noisy offset litho printing machine, a beast from a bygone age, and me. The head's secretary and I printed masses of documents. I cleaned up after her considerable mess, and mine. The cleaning solvent used on the ink rollers, perchloroethylene, was in a five-litre tin with a skull and crossbones on it and recommendations for good ventilation. The window was a slit, nine feet up. This fluid is used in dry cleaners' with strict health and safety rules.

Previous secretaries had lasted a year; I lasted two, with frequent weekend migraines, until my GP said Quit. Health and Safety came to measure air levels, they were a fraction below the legal limit. This scared Major G the Bursar – who insisted I was work shy and it wasn't the machinery – so much that he ditched the offset litho the week after I left. My replacement said "Oh you needn't show me that, they're getting a new machine next week."

It was 1983. At once I moved to a job at Trinity Theological College in a light, clean, airy office. I hoped my health would improve.

Despite being so happy there, after three years, my health had not bounced back. In 1986 I sadly left Bristol and everyone I knew in Bristol. Aunt Alix and Uncle Tom gave me sanctuary in their home in Langford Budville near Wellington for a while. Allergy tests revealed 134 allergies and counting, especially to chemicals. I advertised for jobs in The Lady, and went for several interesting interviews, including a memorable weekend in the family wing at Longleat House, but the allergies prevented me from taking the jobs.

So I bought a chalet at Chapel Cleeve then in 1988 a small flat in Minehead. At first it felt like disaster. I thought Minehead was the back of beyond. Yes and no. Yes, it is 25 miles from a motorway; there are more and more people unable to afford food; some are homeless; the young need jobs; affordable housing is scarce; farmers on Exmoor are isolated and struggling; there are many health needs. This is happening all over the country, not only here.

Minehead, though, has many lovely adventurous people who thrive on a challenge. When a problem arises, someone tries to do something about it. This 'can do' attitude has brought about the Hope Centre for the homeless, the Stroke Club, the Food Cupboard, the Minehead Eye for youngsters, the West Somerset Railway – run by volunteers – as a draw for tourists, Foxes Academy for employment, the volunteer-run Regal Theatre, the flourishing U3A, work to restore the Old Hospital, the Business Improvement District Plans and so on. And there's a wonderful health food store, Toucan, which has won a national award for Best Independent Retailer. Even the Minehead Panto, which flourishes from year to year, was started by a former vicar, Rev Chris Soralis. Anyone who wants to can get involved.

I discovered things I could do even with my limited health. I went for lots of walks on Exmoor. I wrote dozens of prayers. I embroidered a large Exmoor banner – suggested by Old Cleeve rector. When I got a bit better I began to attend a lovely warm friendly church. I joined the Mothers' Union which does good work all over the world and we support the women's refuge in Taunton. I did interviews, wrote articles, word-searches and Bible notes for Minehead Matters, our church magazine. I had written letters for Amnesty International almost since it began. Suddenly an active group coalesced around Chris and Christina Lawson when they arrived. I prompt for plays the Barnstormers do at the Regal Theatre. I hear readers in Year 2 at Minehead First School. I have introduced a charity to our church called Amigos – we raise money for a training farm for AIDS orphans in Uganda. Is Minehead the back of beyond? If so, it's brilliant.

God had a hand in this. I had been running away from myself ever since saying no to Kenneth Hyde and to dear Peter. I had run away to Canada though it turned out fairly well. Now it was time to get really sorted. It was the start of a health turnaround.

My mercury amalgam fillings had already been replaced with white composite as this helps people with chemical sensitivities. It was done in two goes by an ordinary dentist. It's now done with much training, protocol and expense.

Valium (for allergies?) was offered me. It went in the bin. Since the exposure to perchloroethylene I still don't cope well with chemicals: perfumes, aftershaves, fabric conditioner, bleach, Dettol, air fresheners, disinfectants, polishes – there are hundreds. Nor NHS chemical-based drugs.

I discovered all sorts of complementary therapies, some of them really helpful; aromatherapy, acupuncture, reiki, homeopathy, crystals, yoga to name a few. In the words of the rector of Old

Cleeve, Hugh Allen, I "beat the gates of heaven". Possibly God found my incessant banging tedious, information rained down on me. It helped having had nurse training.

I found a massive book on nutrition, Paul Pitchford's Healing with Whole Foods, and read it from cover to cover. It drew on oriental and western knowledge of the values of foods, plants, herbs and spices and also stressed the interplay of body and mind. I became much more adventurous with food. Through the year there are at least 42 varieties of vegetable, and 22 of fruit, "richly to enjoy". Organic food has the most minerals and vitamins, I buy as much as I can afford. Processed foods have many chemical additives.

I was told "listen to your body". It is said we have two brains, one in our head, the other in our gut.

Someone introduced me to a person in Minehead who did acupuncture and diet therapy. She said she could help. She did. First, she told me not to eat the most common allergen, wheat. Most of us eat it at every meal, too often. OK, for porridge there's barley, tapioca (ugh), rice, buckwheat, millet, and oats and spelt for those who can deal with gluten. Next, to get rid of candida, a common infection, No sugar, No honey, No fruit. (She was unkindly nicknamed Dr No). And very little fat, to give my liver a rest. Ouch. "Do you want to get better, or don't you?" "Yes, Miss". In a year (with a few lapses at the fish and chip shop down Bampton Street) I lost four stone and felt heaps better.

Worse, a new worry. She said I needed to be aware of electric fields, magnetic fields and radio frequencies, because having become sensitive to chemicals made me more susceptible to these, too.

Bless her, she spoke from her own experience. She was an extreme sufferer which she believed was caused by her childhood in London living a street away from an active radar station during World War Two. Almost everyone she knew on their street became ill. She was a sort of Cassandra or Jeremiah, trying to wake people up to these increasing modern dangers and how to avoid them.

She didn't have a microwave oven or a mobile phone or a cell phone or a computer or TV. When a satellite went up at Cape Canaveral she felt it. I saw this once, she shook all over like a seizure. I believed all she said, I just didn't want it to apply to me. She couldn't go into a building with a hearing loop, there were parts of town and some buildings she wouldn't go near, she couldn't go to the Catholic church. There is a great deal of literature about the effects of modern technology on peoples' health, there's a Dr William Rea in the States who is a leader in the field.

Like some clever people she couldn't understand when others, like me, couldn't keep up with her. It was, "Don't do this, don't go there". I did try to listen, I did learn, I don't have a microwave or a mobile phone or a smart meter and can only sit at my laptop a few hours a day on a special frequencydiverting cushion. I just wished I could hide under the rug and it would go away.

We fell out over something trivial. Ungrateful as I am, it was a relief and a blessing.

Almost at once someone found a person in Taunton who had cured herself of leukaemia, and was helping people with Lyme's disease, cancer, organophosphate poisoning and other things. Having trained as a beautician, she discovered that skin problems sometimes came from something deeper. She got interested, travelled to the States and trained with a remarkable herbalist, Hannah Kroeger in Boulder, Colorado. She still does beauty treatments as well. She just loves people. She has a unique method, using herbs, diet, minerals, vitamins, homeopathy, light treatments, etc. Some doctors are interested. It may become mainstream one day. She reckons about 20% of people have compromised immune systems like me.

Her help has been more than I could have asked or imagined. She helps me cope with the electromagnetic problems, so as to be partially normal. Any problem that life throws up she will either tackle or look for an answer somewhere.

She found in several patients, including me, shock buried deep like an invisible splinter. It needs therapy of various kinds or counselling or both to dissolve it. She. treated me for it. It became much less. I just thought I must be a wimp, never getting over the shock of my parents' going. There has been a lot of research in the USA by a Dr Bessel van der Kolk and others around this kind of thing in his Trauma Clinic, because of people who have suffered far more than I can imagine.

On the emotional side of things, although my mother had meant it as an insult, I did need that psychiatrist, or some help. It came. The kind NHS gave me free counselling. Not having to go to work meant time at last to get sorted. A retired priest-cum-psychotherapist, a listener, took over. Having buried so much under the rug, a habit taught by Aunty G, I began to get the hang of talking a bit. Wonderfully, various cousins and friends gave support too.

Out of the blue, the best thing of all. In 1996 my old friend Mary Lawson wrote from Toronto urging me to contact the Children's Aid in case Catherine might be looking for me. In Canada, when an adopted child wants to find a birth parent, both parent and child have to give written consent before details are given. Over here, it used to be that a child could be given information and might turn up at the birth parent's house unannounced. It happened to a friend, causing grief and heartache. (If this has not been changed, it is high time for someone to reconsider.) As advised, I wrote to the Children's Aid. There was nothing on file but I registered my willingness to be contacted.

Six months later, an A4 envelope with their logo arrived. My smile went twice round my head. The neighbour Rosie Jones asked "Have you won the lottery?" "Better."

God was giving her back.

First there were consent forms, then telephone contact. Catherine Mary had been changed to Katherine Elizabeth. We spoke, excited. I wrote to Bill – her father - who was still at Sick Kids'. He phoned me: "Where is she?" His office was round the corner from her flat, the same post code. He took her out to dinner, was smitten. The Children's Aid were delighted at the success of our all finding one another so happily. It does not always happen. Word got around.

My daughter and I met at Taunton station. It was February and cold. I was huddled in the waiting room with a thriller. She was on the train with a thriller. Neither of us a bit nervous. We picnicked in Wellington Park (given to the town by Thomas Fox, a forbear). I showed her granny's house, Oldway, turned into flats. Coincidences mounted; she loves singing, so do I; she had done a Teaching English as a Foreign Language course and taught in China for 18 months; I had done one; we had both done lifesaving swimming courses. And so on. Wow. She had shortened Katherine to just Kat. Her adoptive mother's name is Katy. This tends to confuse people.

Next time, Kat came with her fiancé, Peter Kennedy. We had a large family bring and share party at West Buckland village hall, everyone wanting to see this new cousin who had been sprung on them (I had told Andrew and Hermione). Her four cousins, Andrew's children, were delighted. Instructed to dress 'with panache' they turned up in overpowering Hawaii style T shirts. A lovely neighbour, Jean Parbrook, made us a huge fruit cake.

Her adoptive mother Katy, a generous soul, always wanted her three adopted children to know their birth parents. With us it happened. Katy is still a lovely friend, wrapped up in her children's lives, sending me enormous parcels at Christmas, from her finds in charity shops. It's like a lucky dip arriving in the post.

Andrew and Hermione went to Kat and Peter's wedding at their church in Toronto. Kat wore my Maltese cross. She outshines me in every way. It's an honour to know her. Her father Bill and his wife Pat are good grandparents, they help the four grandchildren with things like skiing lessons and birthday treats. Kat does upholstery, she has more than enough work. Peter is an actor and a lay reader. The kids are keen on the performing arts. His family, the Kennedy clan, are well known in Toronto.

My Journey in Faith

The lasting appeal of John Bunyan's Pilgrim's Progress is that here is someone the ordinary person can relate to. He sets out on a journey with no idea what he is letting himself in for, only that he wants to leave where he is and to get rid of his burden, which he does. And that is only the start. It turns out to be a long journey. He falls into difficulties time and again and keeps on seeking. Guides come alongside to help his search. Although he is called Christian, he hasn't got it made. Far from it, he is tentative, questioning, feeling his way, asking for help, looking for the Celestial City he has heard of. It pretty much describes my life.

When I was five, outside St John's, Wellington, I asked my mother "Where is God?" She pointed up at the sky. Granny knew God to talk to. We sat in 'her' pew in church, it felt safe and nice. Granny's maid and friend, Louie, gave me a tiny book called 'Little Pillows' by Frances Ridley Havergal, full of gentle Victorian piety for a small child. It is a great treasure.

When my aunt and uncle took us to Meeting in Wellington on Sundays, God was there, too, in the fresh flowers on the table, in the quiet. Aunty Meg read every Sunday from Advices and Queries, wisdom on how to lead a good Quaker life. She took us children into a side room and read to us from Pilgrim's Progress. This we played round the Gerbestone mill pool, where there was a splendid Slough of very muddy Despond. In the house, hanging beside the front stairs, was a life size oil painting of Aunty G's beautiful young mother sitting reverently in a shaft of sunlight in Westminster Abbey.

Our first school, St Katherine's, a Woodard foundation, was 'high' church and spartan. The boarders' airy dormitories had names; Prudence, Fortitude, Patience. The day began with 9 am chapel. After rushing up the quarter mile drive I had to find my buff overall and white veil, put them on, and get to chapel with seconds to spare, to join the twelve boarders in our form. The school hymn was 'Blest are the pure in heart.' It was both a reproach and an inspiration.

At age 13 I was sent to my second school, Sherborne School for Girls, then as now very strong Anglican. There were whole-school prayers on weekdays, house prayers every evening, Sunday morning services either in the Abbey or in school, and on Sunday evenings too. Therefore, many hymns, psalms, Bible readings and sermons permeated our young lives, underpinning academic and sporting excellence. It still is an excellent school, I was very happy there.

My first term – autumn – ended with the school nativity play. We sat in the reverent dark quietly singing O Come, O Come Emmanuel before the blue curtains parted. The headmistress was very keen on drama, she produced it.

She also taught us Scripture by means of many plays she had written about St Paul's travels. Acting them livened up our lessons. For the Oxford and Cambridge School Certificate our set text was Isaiah. It wasn't suitable for her plays, we did it 'neat'.

The language blew me away (no wonder Handel set great chunks of it to music in Messiah).

"In the year that king Uzziah died, I saw the Lord, high and lifted up, and his train filled the temple" (CH 6). Oh wow. And "I will give you beauty for ashes, the oil of joy for mourning, the spirit of praise for heaviness..." (Ch 6l). We also 'did' Mark's gospel, the story so immediate and urgent, Jesus loving, healing and teaching and inspiring people, it could have happened yesterday.

I sang in the school choir. "Jesu, joy of man's desiring" was an intoxicating introduction to Bach's harmonies. My friend Jean's mother Monica, who came every term with food and funny poems, said when she got to heaven she hoped she would sing Bach for ever.

We were confirmed in the Abbey, with a bishop and candles, a special tea and other peoples' parents. I think Isaiah had done the confirming for me.

I loved school.

My parents were on the boat steaming Home, they arrived just after I left school.

It went very wrong very soon. The faith of my school days disappeared. Nobody thought of asking God to help. Granny would have but she had died two years earlier. I can remember it like yesterday and wish I couldn't. I lost a lot. There are still bits to pick up.

In London I went with Anne and Ann to the youth group at St Mary Abbot's, Kensington because it was expected of me. We fell in with a bunch of very nice physics students from Imperial College, Ann got engaged to one of them. We went to a weekend retreat at Pleshey, the former home of the writer Evelyn Underhill. It was cold, silent, and holy, very safe. I would have liked it to go on and on. I needed safe.

In Toronto, on my own and needing company, I found a good church group to mingle with. We went away on camping weekends and played tennis. Since childhood, used to being the insignificant one in a large household, I felt safety in numbers, where I could blend into the background and not be singled out. I had, I thought, left family problems behind.

One of our nursing classmates belonged to the Salvation Army. Unlike our family, rooted in one town for generations, she and her family were moved every four years, yet she felt safe, due to her faith. She met every practical setback with an uproarious sense of fun, loads of common sense, and an utter dependence on prayer. God was her best friend, she talked to him a lot. Oh. Prayer. About anything. Anything? To a buttoned-up Anglican, this was new and refreshing.

We went to some Pentecostal tent rallies. These were a bit too far out for me but a learning experience. One young man fell down overcome by the Spirit and nobody picked him up for ten minutes. We disgraced ourselves by getting the giggles. I like a God who laughs.

On my return to England it seemed I had only shelved my inward feelings of guilt about my mother plus a lot else from that bad time.

In Bristol, my bedsit in a Georgian house was two doors from Redland Meeting. So convenient on Sundays. They were most welcoming.

Then, on a wet Saturday, the Jesus I had been circling around for most of my life became central to it and has remained there. At Redland Parish Church I found friendliness and kindness. Besides being vicar's secretary, I joined a home group. We studied either some part of the Bible suggested by the vicar or something we chose. The same people were there for years so we got to know each other very well. Our faith grew as we learned from each other.

Writing this story has helped me take a grown-up look at my parents. After the first lovely time in India we had so little time together and what we had was so fraught. It is time to understand how much it has shaped my life; to take responsibility for my share of the misunderstandings, and to forgive them and myself.

When telling people that I'm a Christian, the last thing I want to do is put them off. I wish people could catch a glimpse of the sort of love, help, security, joy and endless discovery it gives me. I don't know if I consistently toe the line. Everyone is different, unity is not uniformity. What I do know is I'd be nowhere without my faith. I believe God made and loves every human being; that no matter how innocently, purposefully or evilly we mess up, His wounded love is still there. That prayer is us talking to Him (any pronoun is inadequate) because He wants our friendship and like a good friend enjoys the to and fro of conversation.

I believe that God sent Jesus to show us what love is and does, and that mankind thrives wherever there is that kind of selfgiving love. There's an old joke; "Jesus is the answer" - "What's the question?" I think it's all questions. From the day we're born to begin our life's journey to the day we die, our lives are full of questions and learning, and through prayer and listening to God we are given surprising answers. Jesus asked questions too, remember. When prayer becomes a daily habit, like breathing, and as much a necessity, life becomes charged with wonder, fun and purpose.

I'm trying not to get tangled in amateur theology, I only want to explain how I feel.

One metaphor for life is a journey or a quest. When I set out on my journey, what I originally wanted was: perhaps a glittering career in the Foreign Office, a nice husband, a thatched house, 2.5 children, a golden retriever, a 'harmless necessary cat', plus good works and perhaps travel. Instead the complete disaster of my parents' return scuttled the lot. In came self-doubt and crippling guilt and a quest to discover why. I did jobs and found out things I needed to know. I did other jobs and discovered a whole world of good people and interesting things. In all this, I had a stubborn wish that I could come out the other side. Gloriously, I feel I have. Prayer 61 has removed a mountain of guilt. Being myself is not a crime nor a betrayal of all the money my parents spent on me. Being oneself is a duty and a joy, a chance to serve and cherish others using whatever gifts God gives us each. "God has no grandchildren", he loves each one of us and wants us each to be happy and fulfilled by being the best we can be.

I hope this small piece of family history and personal experience may interest or help someone else.

www.ingramcontent.com/pod-product-compliance
Lightning Source LLC
Chambersburg PA
CBHW061053050726
47592CB00004B/1657